HAIRCARE
UNDER HIJAB

BY

NATASHA SOMALIA

FIRST AND FOREMOST, I THANK ALLAH FOR GUIDING ME TO ISLAM WITHOUT ALLAH I AM NOTHING!

To all the Muslimahs across the world, who partake in the same daily hair issues as myself this is for you. Thank You for allowing me to maintain and nurture your hair.

To my children Erica, Felicia, Tyriq, Abdullah and Ayyub you all keep me motivated I love you all.
LaVerne A. Davis my mother, you raised me to believe in myself and my abilities, to be strong even amid hardship. I love you for all that you have instilled in me.
William J. Hill my father, I know you would be so proud of me for not giving up!
All my clients, friends, and family that have supported me as well as anyone who has purchased this book!
Thank You!

TABLE OF CONTENTS

FORWARD

Everyone wants healthy hair but no one knows how to get there. With so many products to choose from social media on overload with advice. Hence is why I felt the need write a guide for Muslimahs for starters alhumdulilah I'm a Muslimah so I can relate to some of the struggles that you may have faced or facing now. I'm a licensed professional a haircare specialist with 26 yrs. of doing hair when I say doing hair I mean I touch all different textures daily. I hear the needs of my clients. I've worked diligently to have haircare products for women like you women like me Muslimahs who cover their hair. Let this book be a guide for your Healthy Hair Journey. I have dispelled some of the myths and give you some solutions as well. Enjoy.

Natasha Somalia

"HEALTHY
HAIR IS
GOOD HAIR
YOU HAVE
TO DO
WHAT'S
BEST FOR
YOU AND
DEFINE
YOUR OWN
BEAUTY"

-*Natasha Somalia*

Chapter 1

HIJAB & MATERIAL

My fellow hijabis welcome I know that this is the main topic for everyone, so I'm excited to have it as the first chapter. We all have this in common we cover our hair, and there are tons of materials and fabrics to choose from with an array of fashion and style. Now how it affects our hair will depend on our hair texture and type that's what separates all of us for none of us have the same DNA, so this will be an individual choice of choosing the fabric that works best for you and your hair. With so many beautiful options this can be a hard task however it all depends on if you're going to the gym, the office or a special event, the material will change depending on the occasion. So here are just a few of my favorite materials that I use on a daily basis depending on my activity for the day.

Silk It is one of the strongest natural fibers Silk is very gentle to the skin and hair-- it's protein fibers are like that of hair—I recommend silk for women who may suffer from allergies to other fabrics.
You will also need to wear an Under scarf because of the slippage

Chiffon A smooth material made of medium weight polyester and perfect for everyday use.
You will need to wear an underscarf because of the slippage.

Georgette Semi-transparent fabric with a grainy surface due to the weft threads. With so much twist in the yarns, this material has a natural bounce. Excellent for lightweight, flowy hijab especially fancy for special occasions.
You will need to wear an under scarf if it's too transparent

Jersey Knit Very soft and stretchy does not snag or cause damage to your hair. It's one of my favorites not only no need for an underscarf but no need for pins!

Viscose Very soft to touch another one of my favorites and you can compare it to Rayon this will not snag your hair.

.

"LOVE YOUR HAIR"

-Natasha Somalia

Chapter 2

WUDU GHUSL

I took my shahadah in 2006 and only had to make wudu and ghusl from my menses, but in 2007 my hair totally changed. Not only did my hair change but the products that I would use on my clients would change as well. In 2007 I started mixing oils butter and shampoo trying to figure out what my hair was missing. Everything that I had previously used just was not working with my new routine of more frequent ghusl. My zawj said "Are you still going to give your clients the same advice" with a crazy look on my face I replied "NO" at that moment I knew that I had to create something exclusively **FOR COVERED HAIR.**

MY REGIMEN AFTER WUDU
My hair is color treated so after wudu I always make sure I have some Cashmere Oil handy it's very light, and it comes in travel size, so I don't leave home without it.

MY REGIMEN AFTER GHUSL
Daily I use the Chamomile Cleansing Conditioner next I use the Cream leave in hydration then the Cashmere Oil

Once a month I shampoo with Cache Replenishing Shampoo Caviar Replenishing Conditioner and the Clear protective serum before either blow drying or two strand twist.

"YOUR
PERCEPTION
OF BEAUTY IS
YOU IT'S IN
THE MIRROR"
-*Natasha Somalia*

Chapter 3

CHEMICAL TREATED HAIR

Now I know a lot of curly girls, however, there are some woman who still use to get relaxers or texlax their hair or even get a texturizer, so I just wanted to break down what they all do. First, they are all chemicals and should be done by a licensed professional I just need you to know the difference in the treatments for they do affect your hair under your hijab and without proper care and upkeep your hair will break become dry and damaged.

RELAXER This is the use of chemical hair relaxing products that take overly curly hair turning it into straight form. The result is hair that is straight, in an irreversible way. A professional will check the texture, porosity, elasticity, and damage if any is present in the hair before the start of your service.

TEXLAXING This is a process where hair during the relaxing process, is deliberately under processed. The result is that the hair after the relaxing process does not completely straighten out. This is a process that especially uses the products employed in the relaxing process, but on a minimal level, with the intention of only slightly straightening the hair. So, keep in mind that Texlaxing is still a chemical

treatment and the hair should still be taken care of the same way that you will take care if you are fully relaxed which some stylist will not tell you during your consultation process and unfortunately, hair becomes very dry and brittle and breaks.

TEXTURIZING The best way that I can describe texturizing is using a mild relaxer just to loosen your curls. Texturizers, are applied on the hair in the same way relaxers are, since, just like relaxers, they are a creamy consistency, and they qualify, when applied to the hair, as a chemical-based process. So, when someone tells you, they have a texturizer, not a relaxer you can inform them they have given you the wrong information.

MAINTENANCE OF CHEMICAL TREATED HAIR

Taking care of relaxed hair under hijab requires frequent bi-weekly visits to the salon at the minimum as well as on schedule touch ups daily moisturizing techniques such as sealing your ends at night the Cashmere Oil is excellent for that purpose you want to apply the Cashmere Oil to the last 2-3 inches of your hair ensuring that your ends are fully covered but do it lightly you don't want your hair to be too heavy. You also want to make sure that you sleep with a satin/silk bonnet or have the same material in a pillowcase.

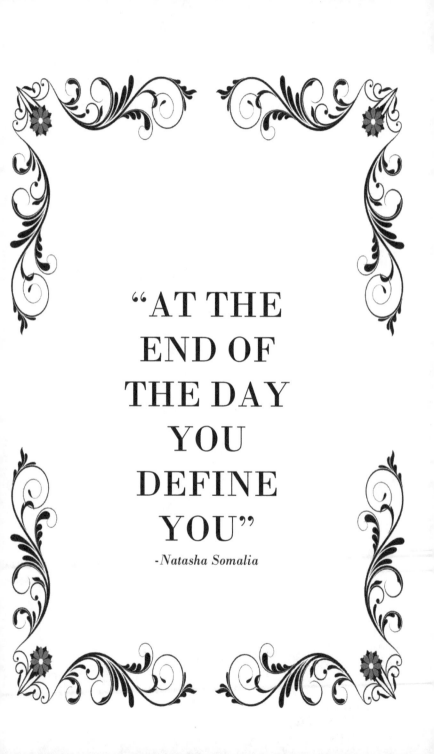

"AT THE
END OF
THE DAY
YOU
DEFINE
YOU"

-Natasha Somalia

Chapter 4

NUTRITION

We have all heard that statement "You are what you eat" I'm going to start this chapter by dispelling the myth that what you put on your hair makes it grow! **NOT TRUE** it's what you put in your body that makes it grow I can't express enough it has always been the number one question! Uhkti guess what if you want healthy luxurious hair then you must make changes to your diet.

What you put on top of your hair maintains the health on the outside.

We all get nervous when someone says, "what have you been eating" I know that you're thinking how could what I eat for breakfast lunch and maybe even dinner have such an impact on my hair health.

First, on our list, we have good ole WATER WATER WATER H2O H2O H2O not drinking water can lead to some serious health problems. Water is needed for your overall essential health as well as your hair so think about it this way if your body is dehydrated how will that affect your hair? Need some help? You need to drink more water, or it will lead to dry, brittle strands! No matter what you do you have to have a nutritious diet especially if you say

You want this healthy hair. So, make the change! You're going to love the results! When you drink your, water eats your fruit and veggies you produce pure beauty benefits not just for your hair but your skin and body as well.

Eat foods that are rich in proteins and vitamins. I will recommend that you add some of these to your daily consumption.

- Raisins
- Whole-grain bread
- Bran cereal
- Brown rice
- Green beans
- Green leafy veggies
- Barley oats
- Whole wheat
- Brazil nuts, Almonds & Walnuts
- Dried fruit
- Bananas
- Spinach
- Salmon
- Red lentils

So here are some of my favorite nutritious ways to get what I need so as you read on you'll see the delicious salad that I made!

Spinach has a very high iron content, and it helps to carry oxygen to the hair follicles. Which is why you will notice that it's in most of my smoothies! Yummy! Whether you drink it or eat it spinach is a great way of getting the nutrients into your diet. Outside of Iron spinach is loaded with vitamins B, C, and E as well as potassium calcium Omega 3 and magnesium which are all great for healthy hair.

Sweet potatoes Yummy! Not only can you use as a hair mask but if you are suffering from dry scalp or skin sweet potatoes are packed with nutrient called Beta-carotene which turns into Vitamin A so if dandruff is a problem for you add more beta-carotene to your diet.

I know that some muslimahs have decided to go vegan but for those who aren't poultry adds a very high level of protein. Protein strengthens the hair in so many ways however if you are vegan you can add lentils to your soup or salads. Not only are lentils a great source of protein but they are a good source of biotin and zinc. If you are struggling with brittle hair add more protein to your diet.

For the vegan's flaxseeds is an excellent way to get your essential fatty acids

Salmon salmon salmon with a nice spinach salad is my go-to meal especially during the month of Ramadhan for iftar salmon is a great source of omega 3 which have anti-inflammatory properties

and what it does for your hair helps open the hair follicles, so your hair or scalp isn't dry and dull looking. So, you want to also add some carrots in that salad we've always known that carrots are great for our eyes however they are loaded with Vitamin A which is where you get that shine from adding that natural oil that your hair loves. This is going to be such a tasty salad because I'm going to add some eggs just for that extra biotin boost and finish my topping with a few walnuts. Walnuts are an excellent source of Vitamin E you will know if you are Vitamin E deficient if your hair snaps or breaks off easy.

VITAMINS

Taking supplements|nutrients is a great way to boost your hair growth, and if you think I'm going to say hey ladies this is it right here the answer to all of your growth problems, then I'm sorry only taking vitamins is not the answer. However, I always recommend my clients to get their levels checked especially for Vitamin D being that we wear Hijab we aren't exposed to a lot of sunlight, so our Vitamin D level is usually low and when that level is low you can lose patches of hair subsequently causing Alopecia. So, I made sure I developed a tasty way for Muslimahs to get that from the D3 gummies which many of my clients are having great results with.

I also know that Biotin is a great source. By receiving this vitamin through your body, it gets deep to the root of things by

- Preventing Breakage
- Accelerating growth
- Prevent Brittleness

So, I formulated the Biotin strawberry gummy which has NO GMO or GELATIN and those I can't keep enough on the shelf. Just remember only to take as many as directed your body can only absorb so much at once. You can't rush it HAIR GROWTH IS A PROCESS!
THERE ARE NO SHORTCUTS!!!

Knowing what's going on with your body has a major impact on your hair. Adding supplements is always good not only for your hair but your overall health as well, but it's not the final key. You still have to trim, moisturize, and care for your hair on the outside having a balanced nutritional diet with an awesome regimen are key!

VITAMINS & NUTRIENTS PROVIDE
- Thickness
- Prevent hair loss
- Strengthen Strands
- Provide Suppleness

Always remember that consistency is key! You have to be committed if you want to see reasonable results and trust me you will love the results!

There are time when our daily schedules may not permit us to make that salad, so you can always take supplements to make sure your body is receiving nutrients in some form. Here are a list of vitamins and what they do for your health and your hair.

- **VITAMIN B1** – Thiamine

  YOUR HAIR} A protein builder that helps give hair shine, volume and good texture; Enhances circulation to bring nutrients to the scalp.

  YOUR HEALTH} Crucial in the digestion process for converting glucose into energy; Supports a healthy nervous system and provides good muscle tone; The "morale vitamin" that promotes positive mental attitude

- **VITAMIN B2** – Riboflavin

  YOUR HAIR} Stimulates health and growth of hair, nails, skin, and eyes by bringing oxygen to body tissues; Can help eliminate dandruff; May aid in preventing loss

YOUR HEALTH} Helps create energy from food by breaking down and using carbohydrates, fats, and proteins. Needed for red blood cell formation, antibody production, and cell respiration and growth. Activates the powerful antioxidant glutathione in the body to battle toxic chemicals and free radicals.

- **VITAMIN B3** - Niacin amide

  YOUR HAIR} Supports healthy hair by helping digestion and improving circulation.

  YOUR HEALTH} Necessary for healthy nervous systems and brain functions; May be effective in lowering cholesterol levels in the blood; May help ease or prevent severe migraine headaches.

- **VITAMIN B5** - Pantothenic Acid

  YOUR HAIR} Helps produce full, healthy hair by stimulating vitamin utilization and releasing energy from food; With folic acid and PABA, can help restore natural hair color; May aid in preventing hair loss.

  YOUR HEALTH} Helps build energy by working to burn fats, carbohydrates, and proteins; Stimulates adrenal glands to produce cortisone and adrenal hormones for healthy skin and nerves; Known as the "anti-stress" vitamin for its role in helping the body produce antibodies and withstand tension and anxiety.

- **<u>VITAMIN B6</u>** – Pyridoxine

  YOUR HAIR} Supports the growth of red blood cells that are important for healthy hair and scalp maintenance; Helps prevent dandruff; Aids in preventing hair loss.

YOUR HEALTH} Facilitates the release of glycogen for energy from the liver and muscles;

Involved in more bodily functions than any other nutrients, but easily lost during improper weight-loss dieting, pregnancy and the use of oral contraceptives.

- **<u>VITAMIN B12</u>** – Cyanocobalamin

  YOUR HAIR} Required for red blood cell formation to help maintain healthy hair and scalp; Useful in eliminating and preventing dandruff.
  YOUR HEALTH} Assist in proper digestion, absorption of food, protein synthesis and metabolism of carbohydrates and fats; Helps iron function in the body; Improves memory, concentration, and balance; Maintains fertility; The only vitamin with essential mineral elements.

- **<u>BIOTIN</u>**

  YOUR HAIR} Helps improve hair quality; Will aid in preventing hair loss. **This vitamin is available in a gummy form**

www.natashasomalia.com

24

YOUR HEALTH} Essential for metabolism of carbohydrates, fats, and protein; Aids cell growth; Important in the utilization of B vitamins

- **FOLIC ACID**

  YOUR HAIR} Helps maintain healthy hair and skin.

  YOUR HEALTH} Required for energy production and red blood cell production; Aids in protein metabolism; Important for production of DNA and RNA

- **D3- Cholecalciferol**

  YOUR HAIR} D3 will help create new follicles - little pores where new hair can grow.

  YOUR HEALTH} Your body must have vitamin D to absorb calcium and promote bone growth. Too little vitamin D results in soft bones in children (rickets) and fragile, misshapen bones in adults (osteomalacia). You also need vitamin D for other important body functions. Not having enough can lead to major hair loss

AS MUSLIMAHS THIS VITAMIN IS VERY IMPORTANT BEING THAT WE WEAR HIJAB WE ARE NOT IN DIRECT SUNLIGHT LEAVING US DEFICIENT YOU CAN ORDER THIS VITAMIN

WWW.NATASHASOMALIA.COM

25

- **<u>INOSITOL</u>**

- YOUR HAIR} Helps improve skin health, hair shine, and body; May aid in preventing hair thinning and loss.

- YOUR HEALTH} Aids in fat metabolism and helps reduce cholesterol

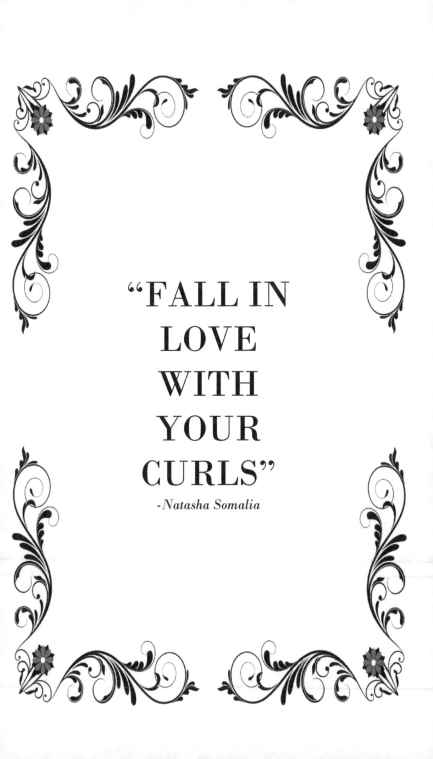

"FALL IN
LOVE
WITH
YOUR
CURLS"

-Natasha Somalia

Chapter 5

HAIR SMOOTHIE FOR HAIR GROWTH

Yummy yummy yes, these smoothies supply you with great nutrient benefits try a few and watch the change….

INGREDIENTS
1 cup spinach
1/2 cup frozen mixed berries
1 Tbsp. chia seeds
1 cup blueberries
1/2 banana
1/2 cup coconut milk/water

INGREDIENTS
1/2 ripe avocado
2 cups spinach
1 cup raspberries
1 cup strawberries
2 Tbsp. chia seeds
2 cups coconut milk/water

INGREDIENTS
1 cup kale
½ cup almonds
1 banana
1 small sweet potato (cooked)
2 cups coconut milk/water

INGREDIENTS
1 cup of spinach
½ cucumber
1 tablespoon of Honey
1 green apple

INGREDIENTS
1 cup kale
½ cup spinach
1 cup pineapple
½ green apple
1 cup low-fat milk
½ tsp turmeric
½ tsp honey

INGREDIENTS
3 Carrots
1 Apple
1/2 Cucumber
2 Celery Sticks

INGREDIENTS
1 cup spinach
2 guavas
2 kiwis
½ cup blueberries

INGREDIENTS
1 green apple
1 carrot
3-6 strawberries

INGREDIENTS
2-3 tbsp. peanut butter
1 banana
a handful of walnuts
1 cup coconut milk/water

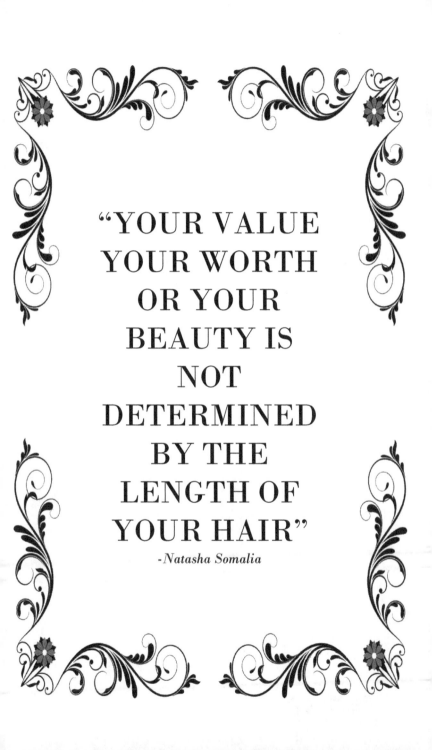

"YOUR VALUE
YOUR WORTH
OR YOUR
BEAUTY IS
NOT
DETERMINED
BY THE
LENGTH OF
YOUR HAIR"

-Natasha Somalia

Chapter 6

CONDITIONING

Conditioning?
What's the first thing that comes to your mind? Sitting longer under the dryer? Will my hair feel different? How much is this going to cost? Does my hair need this? Can I over condition my hair? What's the difference between Conditioner and Deep Conditioner? What's the proper way to condition my hair?

Deep conditioning your hair is one of the most adequate ways to obtain healthy hair and reach your goals.

Dry unconditioned hair can cause breakage up the hair shaft. Especially if you're making a ghusl three or more times a day. So, maintaining moisture under your hijab (khimar) is such a high-priority.

Sadly, using the basic conditioner that comes with the matching shampoo is not as effective as other conditioning treatments. Now I'm not saying to throw out your whole stock of conditioner. I just need you to understand all aspects of conditioning.

Your hair depends on moisture to prevent breakage and increase that lustrous shine.

Maintaining the moisture is the key to keeping your ends maintained and retaining length.

You may have heard me say hair care and wellness go hand in hand well it does the same way increased water consumption provides numerous benefits to the body conditioning treatments provide an immense amount of benefits to the hair.

Proper conditioning routines will add the needed strength and softness, but inadequate conditioning will continue to have your hair feeling dry and brittle.

METHODS OF CONDITIONING

What is a Pre-Poo? If you have ever caught me LIVE via Facebook or Instagram amid doing a conditioning treatment you may have heard me mention the term Pre-Poo. Pre-pooing is the process when you put conditioner on the hair before shampooing it.

I see women first hand right after the braids are out right after weeks of ghusl right after a vacation from swimming.

I know you may be thinking conditioning before shampoo yes because pre-pooing conditions the cuticle, so this process minimizes shedding and breaking since the hair is smoother your hair is more manageable, it makes it easier to work through your hair with less breakage.

PRE-POO

- Excellent for dry, tangled hair
- Minimum indirect heat {steaming} needed
- Leave in for 10-15 minutes {rinse out}
- Makes hair more manageable
- Bottle reads, pre-poo
- Instant results

HOW TO PRE-POO

- Saturate the hair
- Apply a handful or two of CITRUS from roots to ends
- Section hair into 4 or more sections
- De-tangle each section with a wide tooth comb
- Wrap hair with plastic wrap or cover with a plastic cap
- Sit for 10 min up to 15 mins
- Rinse then follow with shampoo and conditioner of choice

The **basic conditioner** is the one that usually comes with the shampoo. See I told you not to throw it out. You need to condition your hair after every shampoo. Conditioning your hair helps you achieve vitality and suppleness.

Basic Conditioner

- Excellent for fine, oily hair
- No heat needed
- Leave in for three to five minutes {rinse out}
- Makes hair softer
- Bottle reads, conditioner
- Lotion like

HOW TO BASIC CONDITIONER

- After shampooing with the shampoo of choice
- Rinse the shampoo completely out
- Apply enough conditioner on the hair to completely cover and saturate the hair
- De-tangle with a wide tooth comb
- Rinse with cool water. Cool water helps to seal the cuticle.

Deep conditioning makes the hair shinier, more supple and softer than a regular conditioning session. You want to take a lot of notes here! Deep conditioning is CRUCIAL for the Hijab

Why should I deep condition? Remember what you're trying to accomplish with your hair! Remember you made a commitment to have healthy hair, so you want to make sure you're keeping it restored, so it's able to hold up against wudu ghusl as well as the fabric from your khimar so keeping that in mind you'll be able to achieve the following

- Peace of mind for the detangling session
- Increase suppleness to the hair
- Improve the manageability of the hair
- Retain moisture

What type is best for your hair you ask? Well, that all depends on the type of results that you want to achieve. You may need to Replenish the Moisture, so I would recommend the Caviar Replenishing or you might need strengthening I would suggest the Shea Butter and Argan Masque. You need to know what your hair needs, and that's what matters the most just keep in mind that deep conditioning is one of the foremost greatest things that you can do for your hair. Next is how often? What is too much?

Everyone's hair is different, so I like to recommend weekly or a bi-weekly routine. For the Hijabi that must make Ghusl 4 times, a day weekly would be best for her. Also, knowing that your diet greatly affects your hair drinking plenty of water and staying hydrated is an added plus! When choosing a deep conditioner pay close attention to what works for your hair, it may be a costly conditioner that will last longer since its getting the job done while something less expensive won't' penetrates as much as you like. Beware of over-conditioning! I know you ladies love to leave a deep conditioner on your hair for hours at a time for various reasons. While conditioning is good for the hair, too much of a good thing is not always better. Yes, your hair will be softer but softer can also be weaker.

Deep Conditioner

- For all hair types
- Makes hair less dense, radiant
- Steam or medium heat
- Rich & Creamy

How to Deep Condition

- Shampoo
- Apply evenly and not just in a ponytail method! Get the middle!
- Section depending on length and thickness you may need more sections
- Detangle with wide tooth comb be gentle!
- Relax this is a process if you want to see results take your time most deep conditioning sessions last 20-45minutes
- Bring on the heat
- Rinse with cool water

Now on to the next! I told you this is amazing to be able to break this information down to you! So, what is a **Leave in Conditioner?**

A leave-in conditioner is like Icing on a cake. Lotion on the skin. Do you need it all the time? You may but that all depends on your hair. There are many types of leave in conditioners some may come in cream for some may be in liquid form The COCONUT Leave in Detangler is excellent for detangling and rejuvenating your curls. Which is great for women who have fine hair or girls who are tender headed! In the cream base form, there's Cream leave in Hydration, and that does exactly what it says it will do add that extra moisture that your hair needs especially if it's coarse. Simply put, if you have the right conditioner, you will be optimizing your hairs integrity. It's imperative to use a leave-in conditioner so that you can achieve detangling with ease, have tamed frizzies, and curls that are oh so lustrous.

Leave in Conditioner

- For all hair types liquid {fine, thin} cream {coarse, thick}
- Protect hair from heat
- No heat needed
- Comes in liquid or cream form

How to Leave in Conditioner

- Shampoo, Condition
- Spray on or Apply cream throughout on damp hair
- Leave in NO need to rinse out
- Style hair as usual

There are numerous products on the market that you can use for any of these conditioning treatments however you must choose which works best with your hair for your regimen. One of my main concerns is that you read the directions and use properly. Conditioning your hair on any level will help you reach your Hair Goals!

Do's

- Focus on your ends
- Follow the directions
- Have balance between your Protein & Moisture
- Deep condition at least once weekly
- Wear a heat cap, use steam for a moisture boost or warm it up if that's required

Dont's

- Don't use your cleansing conditioner or leave in conditioner as a deep conditioner
- If it does not state leave in don't leave it in
- Leave it on longer than the direction states
- Mix brands

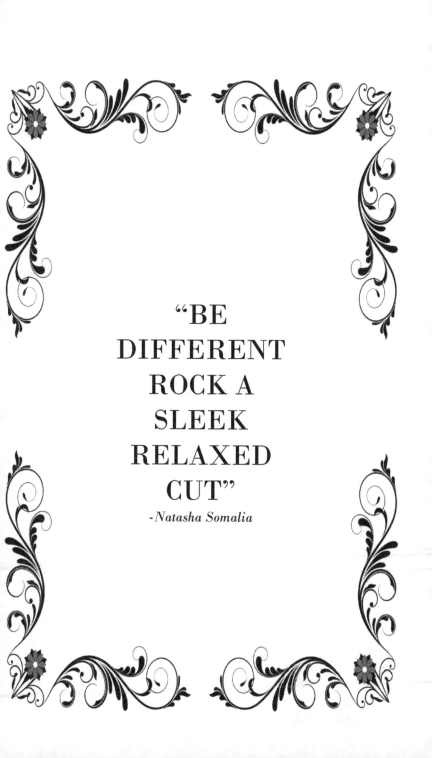

"BE DIFFERENT ROCK A SLEEK RELAXED CUT"

-Natasha Somalia

Chapter 7

CLEANSING

Everyone has their own terminology, and we all know that the hair gurus have come up with so many names in the past 5 years that I try to keep up, but I mostly stay true to my expertise of professional standard so to start off you don't WASH your hair you shampoo your hair or cleanse your hair you WASH your clothes. One of the most famous myths is that dirty hair makes your hair grow! FALSE keeping a clean scalp is a healthy scalp, so ladies please shampoo your hair. When you're making ghusls and leave, your hair damps it starts to smell especially if you sweat a lot. How do I know? I have to shampoo the hair! There are so many shampoos on the market, and I know that you get confused, so I'm going to break them down for you and answer a few questions.

CO-WASHING used by us curly girls it's using a cleansing conditioner to cleanse your hair and scalp, so you don't lose a lot of moisture about 90% of my clients co-wash their hair in between visits. If you co-wash daily at some time, you should use a clarifying shampoo.
To be used as often as you like.

47

MOISTURIZING SHAMPOO a moisturizing shampoo will gently cleanse your hair without stripping all your natural oils. Most moisturizing shampoos are Sulphate Free.
To be used weekly.

CLARIFYING SHAMPOO if you're a curly girl like me and use a lot of products your hair will have a lot of buildups. This is when you pull out the clarifying shampoo for that deep cleanse however a lot of clarifying shampoo contain sulphates. If you're a swimmer, it's the clarifying shampoo that I would suggest.
To be used as needed.

BAKING SODA CLEANSING for those who don't want to use a commercial shampoo yes you can add some baking soda with water, and it will cleanse your hair and scalp however you must be careful over time this can weaken your tresses

FREQUENTLY ASKED QUESTIONS

How often should I shampoo my hair? It depends on your lifestyle also if your natural or chemically treated for naturals my advice is once a week and co-wash daily for chemically treated every two weeks at a minimum. Shampooing your hair too often can lead to breakage and if your hair is color treated the color will fade fast. Just be mindful and see what works best with your hair.

How many times should I shampoo my hair? It depends on your hair and how dirty it is, however, I always like everyone to pay attention to the directions on the bottle. My professional advice is at least 3x's.

Can I just shampoo my hair and not condition? Not you must use a conditioner of some type after your hair is shampooed.

What water temperature should I use? Warm water is best for shampooing and rinsing. However, you should do a cold rinse for the final rinse to lock in the shine.

Should I ever change my shampoo? If you start to feel that your hair feels gooey, it may be that your hair has changed not the shampoo. You might now have color treated hair, so I would suggest using a color treated shampoo or you just may have a lot of buildups and need to clarify.

50

"NO MATTER
THE
TEXTURE
YOUR'E
STILL CUTE
ANYWAY"

-Natasha Somalia

Chapter 8

PROTECTIVE STYLING

What is protective styling? Protective styling is any style that protects your hair from any manipulation.

- Physical Manipulation involves your daily styling which could be combing, brushing, blow-drying or flat ironing
- Chemical Manipulation involves adding Chemical services such as Keratin Treatments, Relaxers or Hair Color
- Depending on your style of choice you can retain more length when your hair is in a protective style in comparison to when it's not.

How do I know if Protective styling is for me?

- Your hair grows to a certain length then breaks
- Your hair has a slow growth rate
- You want to grow out your Chemical Treated hair
- You want to retain length

- You do too much with your hair without giving it any break

Protective Styling is not the only way to achieve long healthy hair. I have seen the benefits of numerous clients that chose this method and had marvelous results. If you're trying to achieve one of these goals, then these methods are for you

PINEAPPLES
This is one of my favorite in the house styles also a great bedtime style, of course, you can't wear a pineapple under your hijab but it's excellent for in the house.

This style is achieved by brushing or finger combing your hair all the way to the top so that it resembles a pineapple

TWO STRAND TWIST
EVERYONES FAVORITE BECAUSE YOU CAN MAKE WUDU AND STILL HAVE A STYLE as well as do a lot of mini styles in between. I recommend two strand twist over braids the hair doesn't have to be pulled tight to achieve this style. It's also a great transitioning style

This style is achieved by taking two strands of hair and twisting them together everyone's main concern is how do they stay if you have curly hair they will automatically stay because of your curl pattern however if your hair is straight you should have flat twist which are done to the scalp and resemble a braid.

BRAIDS

Braids the oldest protective styles and the most convenient for the Muslimah they are such a benefit for your hair mainly because all you have to do is keep them moisturized they can be done in so many patterns your ends are protected especially if you have long hair. There are so many variations of braids you can even create a very elegant style with the French braid which is simple

This style is achieved by using three sections of hair depending on the style that you're trying to achieve. They can be done close to the scalp or individually. If you're on a long hair journey keeping the hair braided is key its low manipulation, and your hair just grows and grows.

"LOVE WATER
SO
REFRESHING"

-Natasha Somalia

58

Chapter 9

TRIMMING vs. CUTTING

The process that some hate and for those who see the benefits they love to get their hair trimmed! I know I know you went to the salon one day and asked for a trim and came home with a new hairstyle. Too often have I heard that story. I'm so sorry that you had that experience, but you should learn to trust again. Try making an appointment for a consultation, so you know what to expect.

It takes understanding your hair to make sure it's in a healthy state. Just think about everything you put your hair through braids, constant ghusl and wudu it needs to be trimmed regularly to keep it healthy. Your hair is like a plant it grows, falls out and replaces itself. However, the hair that was once at the root has traveled such a distance, and now it needs to be trimmed. I know that you may never have experienced the length that you may currently have, but you want more length not split ends, so it's best to make sure that you keep up with those trims.

At this time, you really don't want to think about the length but the overall health of your hair. In the long run, you're going to see that it's what's best for your

hair. Think of it this way this is a new journey, and it's out with the old and in with the new.

Now a haircut is completely different you get a haircut when you want a style, or you're doing a BIG CHOP. However, some people like to get a good cut when the seasons change they want a different look. That's always your decision.

HOW OFTEN SHOULD I GET TRIMS?

The recurrence of trims depends on how healthy your hair is from the start. If you have been ignoring it and it's dry or damaged, then the scissors are about to become your best friend just keep in mind once you have your regimen and start the results are going to be so rewarding.

HOW CAN I TELL IF IT'S TIME TO TRIM?

Have you ever noticed that your hair isn't holding a curl? Or it's very hard to detangle especially if you have single strand knots and you need to use smaller and smaller sections just to detangle. You can notice single strand knots by the feel of your hair it will be rough it's easily noticed when you do a twist out if you style your hair in a protective style. You must pay close attention and listen to your stylist she will be able to determine what's best for your hair.

HOW MUCH SHOULD I CUT?

Well if you want to do a dramatic change when you want to have a session with your stylist and think of something tailored for you.

CAN I CUT MY OWN HAIR?

I don't suggest it however many women have had bad experiences and decided to do it themselves I don't recommend it! I just recommend you find a stylist who listens!

My promise to you and those who have had the opportunity to sit in my chair is this! If you trim the dead, lifeless strands off, you'll be one step further to your healthy hair journey!

I will close this chapter by also letting you know that trimming your ends or cutting your hair **DOES NOT MAKE YOUR HAIR GROW**! Your hair grows from within! Trimming the ends allows it not to split up the shaft!

"I SPEND MORE TIME FIXING MY HIJAB THAN MATCHING MY SOCKS"

-Natasha Somalia

Chapter 10

HAIR LOSS THINNING & SHEDDING HAIR

Oh, my gosh Somalia I think I'm going bald look right there do you see it look! I hear this maybe ten times a week. Somalia what's wrong with my hair why is it doing that.

Ok, so there are so many factors to why your hair may be thinning. It can be hereditary or pregnancy a change in medications birth control also scalp conditions like alopecia and the #1 cause STRESS! Or you may be a part of this group excessive pressing of hair which means you use the straightening comb and the flat iron or your braids are too tight or your tying your nikab too tight that it leaves a hole in the middle of your head or your just naturally hard on your hair.

So now we must determine why your hair is thinning. I like to examine what happened three to six months prior to your experience. Once we go through the most likely experiences above then, we start with the solutions.

A lot of women have experienced hair loss at some time during their hair journey. What many women don't know is the difference between serious hair loss natural hair thinning and hair shedding. Most of

the time it's hair shedding which is completely normal.

NATURAL SHEDDING

When you make a ghusl, and shampoo your hair and notice hair in the shower drain or your comb, every single day? That's normal! Everyone's average daily hair shed is anywhere between 100-150 strands per day. It's natural from your hair growth cycle. Your hair grows comes out and replaces itself. Add some Biotin to your daily intake, and you will notice less shedding the Biotin will help nourish the follicles and strengthen your hair! When you give birth, your hair also goes through a phase of shedding and my recommendation for that is to continue your pre-natal vitamin and consult with your physician.

HAIR LOSS

There can be many reasons that you're losing your hair this is when you see it come out in patches! Being that you're a Muslimah and cover you don't get exposed to a lot of sun so you may have a vitamin d deficiency. I strongly recommend taking my d-3 gummies this will give you what you're missing from the sun. When I say patches of hair I speaking on more than 150 strands in your shower or comb a day. This can also be caused by the medications that you take high blood pressure, birth control to name a few you also may have a thyroid condition, and my recommendation would be to consult with your doctor.

HAIR THINNING

Hair thinning can be associated with a few things that may pertain to age as well as your hormones or what you're doing to your hair. If you braid your hair too tight you may develop traction alopecia. If all your relatives are thinning in one spot, then it's hereditary in your genes. Changes to your diet can also change the structure of your hair especially if you have taken nutrients out and not replaced them accordingly.

3 MAIN REASONS WHY YOUR HAIR COMES OUT

1. STRESS I can't say it enough if you are stressed your hair will fall out!
2. Doing too much with your hair and not properly moisturizing and conditioning it. If you have Chemically Treated Hair, you must take care of it.
3. Your body not getting enough WATER or NUTRIENTS you must eat healthy if you want to have Healthy Hair!

"YOU HAVE
TO LOVE
WHO YOU
ARE FOR
WHO YOU
ARE"

-Natasha Somalia

HAIR CARE REGIMEN

Everyone's regimen will not be the same, so you ask me why? Well what your hair may need my hair may have lots of. Your hair may be chemically treated, and mines may be natural your hair can be wavy mines may be straight You may take a ghusl 4 times a day I may only take a ghusl once a month so when a client ask me what do I do to have my hair so healthy everything that I may do for my hair may not pertain to your hair. So, for you to have your own regimen you must take into consideration are you working out daily? Are you going to the salon frequently? Are you doing everything yourself using homemade products etc. etc.

There is something that I know that we all have in common we all COVER our HAIR which means our hair tends to be very dry at times so this regimen that I'm giving is one in general and you can tailor it to your liking. While changing thing up once you start knowing your hair you will see which approach works best for you.

A friend may recommend a deep conditioning treatment that she left on for 30 mins and now you've tried it for 30 minutes and you're a grease ball. So be patient be consistent!

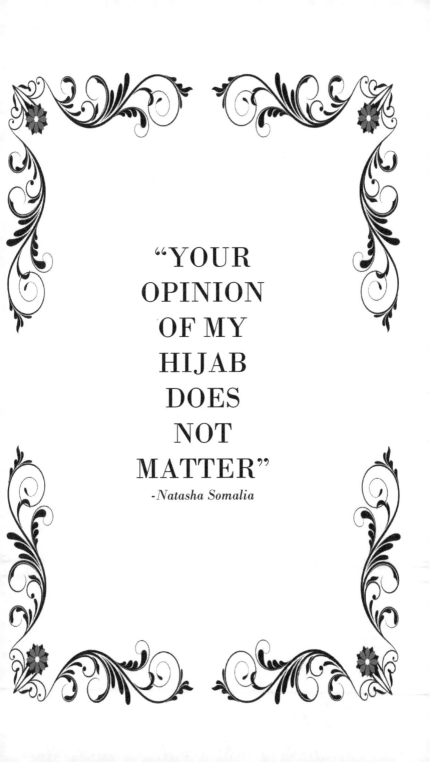

"YOUR
OPINION
OF MY
HIJAB
DOES
NOT
MATTER"
-Natasha Somalia

CLARIFY AT LEAST ONCE A MONTH
CO-WASH IN BETWEEN SALON VISITS
DEEP CONDITION EVERY WEEK FOR 25
MINS WITH STEAM
USE A LEAVE IN DAILY
SEAL ENDS AT NIGHT
WEAR PROTECTIVE STYLES UNLESS IT'S A
SPECIAL OCCASION
HEAT ONLY THREE X'S A YEAR
TRIM AS NEEDED
SLEEP WITH A SATIN BONNET

HAIR CARE STRATEGY

CONSISTENCY IS KEY
EAT HEALTHY
TAKE YOUR VITAMINS
BE PATIENT
KNOW YOUR GOAL
REWARD YOURSELF
HAVE A PLAN
KNOW YOUR WHY

"KINKY
IS NOT
A BAD
WORD"

-*Natasha Somalia*

MY HEALTHY HAIR JOURNEY NOTES

WEEKLY

-
-
-
-

BI-WEEKLY

-
-
-
-

MONTHLY

-
-
-
-

MY HEALTHY HAIR JOURNEY

MY WHY

-
-
-

HEALTHY HAIR GOALS

-
-
-

TIME TO ACHIEVE MY GOAL

-
-
-

AUTHOR BIO

While most young girls were playing with their baby dolls, six-year old Natasha Somalia was using hers to teach herself how to braid hair. In 1991 Natasha Somalia graduated from Dobbins Technical High School in Philadelphia Pa. and had finished the State of Pennsylvania curriculum for Cosmetology and received her License at the age of 17 years old. After working at a few local salons Natasha Somalia quickly
discovered the power of her passion. She saw first-hand the impact she was having on her customers, that she could make them feel better about themselves.
In 1996, Natasha opened her first salon. She was just 23 years old.
What has happened since then has allowed her to live her dreams while doing what she loves making women feel good about themselves.

Hair Care and Texture Management, Natasha Somalia, has interchangeable roles as Creative stylist, Product developer, Top educator, and Business entrepreneur.
Natasha's impeccable reputation for hair care and an academic approach to the study of hair texture, products and styling tools have revolutionized the cutting and shaping of hair for all textures. Natasha's motto is Healthy Hair Is Good Hair letting women know the beauty of what they have.

81

Armed with 26years of professional hair care, business management and marketing experience, Natasha used her savvy business acumen to create two of metropolitan Philadelphia's most highly sought beauty destinations for women. Her expertise also offers effective salon management, marketing practices, revenue growth, profitability and work-life balance instruction to salon owners and stylists Globally.

Natasha Somalia is Founder and CEO of Natasha Somalia Beauty & Business Academy COVERED the salon; Co-Owner and Artistic Director of COVERED BEAUTY Hair Studio in the Philadelphia area; KBBS Educator Developer of For Covered Hair the first Haircare Line formulated specifically for women who cover their hair; in the USA and a proud mother of five children.